THE EVERYDAY
INSTANT POT
COOKBOOK

THE EVERYDAY
INSTANT POT
COOKBOOK

Recipes and Meal Planning
for Every Cook and Every Family

BRYAN WOOLLEY

Racehorse Publishing

Racehorse Publishing books may be purchased in bulk at special discounts for sales promotion, corporate gifts, fund-raising, or educational purposes. Special editions can also be created to specifications. For details, contact the Special Sales Department, Skyhorse Publishing, 307 West 36th Street, 11th Floor, New York, NY 10018 or info@skyhorsepublishing.com.

Racehorse Publishing™ is a pending trademark of Skyhorse Publishing, Inc.®, a Delaware corporation.

Visit our website at www.skyhorsepublishing.com.

10 9 8 7 6 5 4

Library of Congress Cataloging-in-Publication Data is available on file.

Cover photography by Dreamstime
Interior photography by Bryan Woolley
Author photograph by Shaun Anders

Print ISBN: 978-1-63158-312-4
E-Book ISBN: 978-1-63158-316-2

Printed in China

CONTENTS

Soups 49

Meat Entrées 75

INTRODUCTION

Finally, somebody preprogrammed some of my favorite pressure cooking features in a single touch of a button. With all of the new safety features on this electric pressure cooker, it has become a joy to use in the kitchen. I always tell people that pressure cooking was the microwave of the fifties and sixties and was used to speed up food preparation. Unlike a microwave oven, which excites water molecules to cook, a pressure cooker forces super-hot steam into the food from the outside in. Healthy and fast, this method of cooking enables the creation of so many new and wonderful ways of enjoying food.

The Instant Pot is a wonderful kitchen tool, but remember it is a pressure cooker. To truly master pressure cooking one must have a solid understanding of the art of pressure cooking. Many of the recipes in this book use the preprogrammed buttons when convenient—however, not all recipes fit within a single button choice. When you use the preprogrammed buttons, notice they are merely pressure cooking modes preset for convenience. Knowing that these modes can be achieved using the manual selection of low or high pressure opens endless ways of cooking your favorite dishes. There are some selections on the Instant Pot that do not pressure cook and require you to open the steam valve. Be sure to check the directions that came with your Instant Pot to be aware of its specific features.

I'll forever remember the amazing dishes my mom and grandmother created using their pressure cookers that hissed and spat water from the rocker tops. While creating this book my mom and I enjoyed many fond memories of food and childhood culinary favorites. She is my number one inspiration and put countless hours into helping me with this book. Much love and admiration to "Mama Louise" for helping and teaching me to love food and to share that love.

Many people have an instilled fear of using a pressure cooker due to the stories from their childhood. Relax. Just always make sure the pressure cooker is cleaned and maintained as directed by your device's manufacturer and that the gaskets are in good working condition with no cracks or breaks in them. Like any cooking tool, you should always treat it with respect and get to know how it works to ensure your safety.

With all of the incredible safety features in the new electric pressure cookers, I'm convinced you will learn to love your pressure cooker while creating amazing foods for your family and friends. Remember, recipes are merely guidelines, and can be adjusted and adapted to your needs and likes. Whatever dishes you choose to create, have fun, enjoy, and build those lasting memories for your family and friends to cherish through the years.

MEAL PLANNING

Meal planning can be a daunting task for anyone. How many times have you gone to the fridge, opened it up, looked at your food options and wondered, "What am I going to make for dinner?" If you answered yes, you're not alone. Planning out a meal doesn't have to be difficult. Start thinking of meals as individual categories rather than a complete picture. In other words, break down the complexity of meal planning into proteins, starches/carbohydrates, vegetables, fruits, and desserts.

When I look in the fridge, I look to first find a protein (such as beef, chicken, fish, beans, or tofu). After I find a protein for dinner I then look for a starch to go with it (potatoes, rice, bread, or pasta). Once the protein and starches/carbohydrates are selected, I then look for a vegetable (carrots, beans, peas, cauliflower, broccoli, or salad). By breaking a meal down into individual components, the daunting task of trying to figure out what's for dinner becomes attainable and easy.

I've created a week's worth of menu ideas showing how to combine components together to create a full dinner. I also placed a soup option on the meal planning table just in case I decide to make soup instead. If I don't use the soup options, I bump the idea to the next week as I plan out future dinners.

Protein	Starch	Vegetable	Dessert	Soup
Pork Roast	Delicious Mashed Potatoes	Steamed Broccoli	Coconut Cherry Cobbler	Bacon and Corn Chowder
Easy Pot Roast	Country Potato Medley	Beet and Arugula Salad with Bacon	Bread Pudding with Caramel Rum Sauce	Country Beef Soup
Beef Stroganoff	Brazilian White Rice	Steamed Artichokes	Steamed Gingerbread	Spicy Pork Ramen
Sloppy Joes	Refrigerator Pickled Beets	Potato salad	Caramel Rum Sauce with Ice Cream	Split Pea and Ham Soup
Steamed Pork Buns	Basic White Rice	Tri-Bean Salad	Sweet Sticky Rice with Mango	Vegetable Kale Soup

Steak Fajitas	Au-Gratin Potatoes	Quinoa and Asian Pear Salad	Cheesecake in a Jar	Mayan Lime Soup
Sweet and Sour Chicken	Basic Brown Rice	Tri-Bean Salad	Aunt Minnie's Apple Sauce with Sweet Dumplings	White Bean and Kale Soup

When planning a meal, stop looking at the whole picture and start compartmentalizing it into smaller ideas.

1. Choose a protein you already have in your fridge.
2. Match a starch/carbohydrate to the protein.
3. Pair any vegetable or salad to your menu.
4. Create an easy dessert you like.
5. If you choose, make a delicious soup instead.

Once you start simplifying the big picture (dinner planning) to smaller/simpler compartments, meal planning becomes fun, easy and cost-effective. Don't go to the grocery store without a plan or you'll generally spend more money than you need to.

SIDE DISHES

COUNTRY-STYLE POTATOES

Prep. Time: 30 minutes
Serves: 6–8

INGREDIENTS:

6 Klondike potatoes, cut into ¼-inch slices

1 tsp. seasoned salt

2 tsp. black pepper

1 tbsp. Italian seasoning herb blend

⅓ cup finely minced onion

2 tbsp. olive oil

1 cup vegetable stock

DIRECTIONS:

1. Rinse already sliced potatoes.

2. In a large bowl, combine sliced potatoes, seasoned salt, black pepper, Italian seasoning, minced onion, and olive oil. Toss to coat potatoes slices.

3. Spray one large 32-ounce ramekin or three to four smaller (4-ounce) ramekins with vegetable spray. Fit the prepared potatoes into the ramekins.

4. Place steam rack inside Instant Pot. Pour in vegetable stock. Transfer prepared potatoes into Instant Pot and secure the lid.

5. Pressure cook on high for 6–8 minutes, depending on how large you have cut the potato slices (thicker slices require longer cooking time). I like Klondike variety potatoes, because I don't need to peel them.

6. When pressure cooking is finished, release pressure using quick-release method.

7. Serve with your favorite main dish.

DELICIOUS MASHED POTATOES

Prep. Time: 30 minutes
Serves: 8–10

INGREDIENTS:

6–7 medium russet potatoes, peeled and chopped into 1-inch pieces

½ cup vegetable stock

½ cup milk

1 stick butter (8 tbsp.)

2 tsp. onion powder

1 tsp. granulated garlic

1 tbsp. Italian seasoning herb blend

Salt and pepper to taste

DIRECTIONS:

1. Place all ingredients into Instant Pot. Secure lid. Pressure cook on high for 9 minutes.

2. Allow pressure to release slowly. When pressure has released, remove lid carefully.

3. Transfer entire potato mixture to stand mixer. Whip potatoes with a whisk, paddle, or mixer attachment.

4. Adjust salt and pepper as needed.

CHEESY MINI POTATOES

Prep. Time: 30 minutes
Serves: 4–6

INGREDIENTS:

1 cup chicken stock

1 pkg. Klondike Gourmet Medley Potatoes

Vegetable oil spray

1 tbsp. seasoned salt

2 tsp. black pepper

2 cups finely shredded cheddar cheese

DIRECTIONS:

1. Place steam rack inside Instant Pot. Pour in chicken stock.

2. Scrub Klondike Gourmet Medley Potatoes. Place them in the Instant Pot and secure the lid.

3. Pressure cook on high for 5 minutes. Do a quick pressure release.

4. Once pressure is released, remove potatoes and place them on a baking sheet.

5. Using a sharp knife, slice halfway through mini potatoes. Gently press ends toward center of potato to open them.

6. Lightly spray potatoes with vegetable oil spray. Sprinkle with seasoned salt and black pepper.

7. Sprinkle cheese on top of potatoes, gently pressing cheese firmly into the potato slit.

8. Place under broiler until cheese has melted. Serve with your favorite dipping sauce. (I like to serve these as mini appetizers at parties.)

DEVILED EGGS

Prep. Time: 30 minutes
Serves: 12

INGREDIENTS:

1 cup water

12 large eggs

½ cup mayonnaise

¼ cup dill relish

2 tsp. paprika

1 tbsp. yellow mustard,
   optional

2 tsp. salt

1 tbsp. black pepper

Freshly chopped parsley or
   chives, *optional*

DIRECTIONS:

1. Place steam rack inside Instant Pot. Add 1 cup water.

2. Carefully place eggs onto steam rack.

3. Secure lid and pressure cook eggs on high for 5 minutes.

4. Do a quick pressure release. (I like to place a clean kitchen towel over the steam vent to catch any hot water droplets that come out.)

5. Remove eggs and place them in a bowl of cold water to cool them.

6. Peel and slice eggs in half lengthwise, scooping egg yolks into a mixing bowl. Place egg white halves on baking sheet.

7. To the egg yolks, add mayonnaise, relish, paprika, mustard (optional), salt, and black pepper. Stir ingredients together until fully mixed.

8. Carefully spoon yolk mixture into center round of each egg white half.

9. Sprinkle prepared deviled eggs with freshly chopped parsley or chives, if using.

AU GRATIN POTATOES

Prep. Time: 20 minutes
Serves: 4

INGREDIENTS:

3 large russet potatoes

½ cup freshly chopped chives

2 tsp. seasoned salt

1 tsp. black pepper

Vegetable oil spray

1½ cups heavy cream

1 cup water

DIRECTIONS:

1. Peel and thinly slice russet potatoes. Do not rinse them (the potato starch helps thicken the sauce).

2. Place potato slices, chives, seasoned salt, and pepper in a large bowl. Toss to coat potato slices.

3. Spray four 5-oz. ramekins with vegetable oil spray and divide the potato mixture between the prepared ramekins. Press potato slices into them.

4. Carefully pour heavy cream into the ramekins, giving the cream time to fill in around the potato slices.

5. Place steam rack inside Instant Pot and pour 1 cup water into it. Place ramekins onto steam rack.

6. Secure lid on Instant Pot and pressure cook on high for 10 minutes. Let steam release naturally.

7. Once pressure has released, carefully remove the lid and ramekins.

8. Place ramekins on a baking sheet and place them under the broiler to brown the tops of the au gratin potatoes.

BASIC BROWN RICE

Prep. Time: 40 minutes
Serves: 6

INGREDIENTS:

2 cups rinsed brown rice

3½ cups stock or water

DIRECTIONS:

1. Place brown rice and stock (of your choice) or water into Instant Pot and secure the lid. Choose Rice setting. Press start. If you do not have a Rice setting, pressure cook on low for about 30 minutes.

2. Allow pressure to release naturally.

3. When pressure has released, remove lid and fluff with fork.

Note: Brown rice takes longer to cook, because the outer layer of the rice is still intact. You may need to increase cooking time by about 10 minutes when using the manual pressure cooking mode. Otherwise, the Rice mode will automatically adjust cooking time, much like a countertop rice cooker.

BASIC WHITE RICE

Prep. Time: 30 minutes
Serves: 6

INGREDIENTS:

3 cups rinsed white rice

5 cups stock (your choice) or water

DIRECTIONS:

1. Place washed rice and stock (can use water if desired) into Instant Pot.

2. Secure lid and set to Rice mode. When finished, let steam release naturally. If you do not have a Rice setting, pressure cook on low for about 12 minutes.

3. Allow pressure to release naturally.

4. When pressure has released, remove lid and fluff with a fork.

BRAZILIAN WHITE RICE

Prep. Time: 30 minutes
Serves: 6

INGREDIENTS:

2 tbsp. olive oil

½ cup chopped onion

3 garlic cloves, minced

1 cup chopped carrots, peeled if necessary

2 cups rinsed long-grain white rice

3¾ cups stock (your choice)

DIRECTIONS:

1. Heat Instant Pot using Sauté mode. Add olive oil.

2. Add onion, minced garlic, and carrots. Sauté until fragrant (about 3 minutes).

3. Add rinsed rice and sauté with onion mixture until the rice becomes translucent white.

4. Add stock of your choice and secure Instant Pot lid.

5. Choose Rice setting and press start. If Instant Pot doesn't have a Rice setting, pressure cook on low for 12 minutes. Allow pressure to release naturally.

6. Remove lid when pressure has released. Fluff with fork.

THE EVERYDAY INSTANT POT COOKBOOK

COUNTRY POTATO MEDLEY

Prep. Time: 30 minutes
Serves: 6

INGREDIENTS:

1 cup vegetable stock

1 sprig rosemary

¼ cup olive oil

1 pkg. Klondike Gourmet Medley Potatoes (about 4 cups)

1 tbsp. seasoned salt

1 tbsp. ground pepper

1 tbsp. Italian seasoning herb blend

DIRECTIONS:

1. Pour vegetable stock into Instant Pot. Add sprig of rosemary and olive oil.

2. Place steam rack inside Instant Pot.

3. Clean potatoes and place on top of steam rack.

4. Sprinkle potatoes with seasoned salt, ground pepper, and Italian seasoning.

5. Secure lid on Instant Pot and pressure cook on low for 10 minutes. Let steam release naturally.

6. Once steam has been released, remove lid.

7. Serve Country Potato Medley with your favorite dinner.

PARMESAN ARBORIO RICE

Prep. Time: 30 minutes
Serves: 6

INGREDIENTS:

2 cups arborio rice

5 cups chicken or vegetable stock

1 cup grated Parmesan cheese

½ cup freshly chopped Italian parsley

Salt and pepper as needed

DIRECTIONS:

1. Pour arborio rice into Instant Pot. Add chicken or vegetable stock.

2. Secure lid and pressure cook on low for 12 minutes.

3. Let pressure release naturally. Remove lid when ready and stir the rice, testing to make sure it's tender. If the rice isn't tender, pressure cook on low for an additional 5 minutes.

4. Stir in Parmesan cheese and parsley.

5. Add salt and pepper as needed.

PICKLED EGGS

Prep. Time: 1 hour
Serves: Variable

INGREDIENTS:

2 quart jars with lids, sterilized

24 large eggs

1 cup water

4 cups white vinegar

⅓ cup sugar

1 tbsp. yellow mustard seeds

1 tbsp. black peppercorns

2 tbsp. dry dill

4 bay leaves, crushed

1 medium onion, sliced

1 tbsp. seasoned salt

DIRECTIONS:

1. Set clean quart jars aside until ready to use.

2. Place steam rack inside Instant Pot. Add eggs along with 1 cup water. Secure lid and set pressure to high. Cook 5 minutes. Allow pressure to release naturally.

3. Once steam has released, remove lid. Place eggs into bowl of cold water. Set aside.

4. Clean Instant Pot and add the white vinegar, sugar, yellow mustard seeds, black peppercorns, dry dill, crushed bay leaves, onion slices, and seasoned salt. Select Sauté mode, bringing mixture to a boil while stirring.

5. Once eggs have cooled sufficiently to handle, peel and divide them between the clean quart jars.

6. Divide and pour pickling solution between the two prepared jars.

7. If needed, strain remaining pickling solution and finish dividing the herbs and spices between the two jars. (Reserve any extra for a vinaigrette on a salad.)

8. Secure lids on jars. Refrigerate overnight.

9. Keep jars in refrigerator when not using. Will last about two weeks.

10. Serve alone or with your favorite salad.

REFRIGERATOR PICKLED BEETS

Prep. Time: 45 minutes
Serves: Variable

INGREDIENTS:

5–6 medium beets

2 cups water, *divided*

2 cinnamon sticks

5 whole cloves

1 large onion, thinly sliced

2 cups vinegar

½ cup sugar

DIRECTIONS:

1. Trim off beet greens and scrub beets thoroughly.

2. Place steam rack inside Instant Pot. Place cleaned beets on rack.

3. Pour 1 cup water into the Instant Pot. Secure lid.

4. Pressure cook on high for 15 minutes. Use quick-release method to release steam.

5. Let beets cool. Remove outer skins.

6. Slice beets into ½-inch cubes, placing them in a sealable container along with cinnamon sticks, whole cloves, and onion.

7. In a large bowl, whisk vinegar, 1 cup water, and sugar together until sugar has dissolved. Pour over beets. Cover and refrigerate overnight before serving.

8. Will keep about two weeks when refrigerated.

STEAMED ARTICHOKES

Prep. Time: 30 minutes
Serves: 4–6

INGREDIENTS:

Olive oil

8 sprigs parsley

2 sprigs thyme

⅓ cup diced onion

3 garlic cloves, mashed

3 bay leaves

1 lemon, juiced and cut into pieces

1 cup white wine

2 tbsp. butter

4–6 artichokes

7 cups water

¼ cup lemon juice

Salt and pepper to taste

DIRECTIONS:

1. Heat Instant Pot on Sauté until hot. Add just enough oil to lightly coat bottom of pot. When heated add parsley, thyme, onion, and mashed garlic cloves. Sauté for 3 minutes.

2. Add lemon juice, lemon pieces, white wine, and butter to pot. Heat through. Turn off heat.

3. To prepare artichokes, wash them under cold water. Cut stems off close to base and peel the hard outer layer of stem. Pull off small lower leaves. Trim off top of artichoke and snip any remaining sharp points from leaves. If you want to clean out the "choke" part, simply spread open leaves and pull out the "choke." Use a spoon to finish scraping out the hairy inside of the heart. Soak artichokes in lemon water until ready to cook, or they will turn brown. Use 6 cups water and ¼ cup lemon juice to create lemon water.

4. When artichokes are cleaned, place them snugly stem-side down in the Instant Pot. The size of the cooker will determine how many artichokes you process at one time. The snug fit in the pot will help secure them while cooking.

5. Once artichokes are in the pot, add 1 cup water.

6. Secure lid as directed. Cover and set Instant Pot to high pressure for 20 minutes.

7. Allow steam to release naturally.

8. Remove Instant Pot lid. Carefully remove artichokes and season with salt and pepper to taste.

9. Serve with your favorite dips. Artichokes can be served hot or cold.

SALADS

BEET AND ARUGULA SALAD WITH BACON

Prep. Time: 30 minutes
Serves: 4–6

INGREDIENTS:

1 cup water

2 golden beets, peeled and chopped

2 red beets, peeled and chopped

6 cups arugula, washed and dried

1 cup feta cheese

1 cup pomegranate seeds

1 cup chopped walnuts

Fresh Peach Vinaigrette:

1 fresh peach, pit removed

½ cup extra-virgin olive oil

¼ cup balsamic vinegar

¼ cup brown sugar

½ tsp. nutmeg

Salt and pepper to taste

DIRECTIONS:

1. Place steam rack inside Instant Pot. Pour in 1 cup water. Add beets and secure lid as instructed.

2. Set pressure to high and cook for 8 minutes. Quick release pressure as directed by manufacturer. Remove beets from Instant Pot and place in bowl of cold water to cool.

3. While beets are cooling, in a large bowl add arugula, feta cheese, pomegranate seeds, and walnuts. Toss to combine.

4. To make the fresh peach vinaigrette, place the peach, extra-virgin olive oil, balsamic vinegar, brown sugar, nutmeg, salt, and pepper into blender and blend together until smooth.

5. Place the arugula mixture on a large platter and sprinkle with cooked beets. Drizzle salad with enough dressing to coat lightly. Any extra salad dressing can be stored in refrigerator for up to two weeks in an airtight container.

6. Serve salad with your favorite artisanal bread.

TRI-BEAN SALAD

Prep. Time: 1 hour
Serves: 6–8

INGREDIENTS:

1 cup dry cannellini beans (can use great northern beans)

1 cup dry red kidney beans

1 cup dry garbanzo beans

16 cups cold water, *divided*

1 cup finely chopped celery

1 cup chopped kalamata olives

½ cup diced red onion

1 cup freshly chopped Italian parsley

1 tbsp. freshly chopped dill

1 tsp. lemon zest

¼ cup cider vinegar

¼ cup sugar

¼ cup vegetable oil

1 tbsp. Dijon mustard

Salt and pepper to taste

DIRECTIONS:

1. Add dry beans along with 8 cups cold water to Instant Pot. Let beans soak for about 30 minutes.

2. Drain water off beans. Add 8 cups cold water back into pot with beans.

3. Secure lid on Instant Pot. Pressure cook on high for 20 minutes. Let pressure release naturally.

4. Once pressure has released, carefully remove lid of Instant Pot and check beans for doneness. If needed, pressure cook for an additional 5 minutes.

5. Once cooked, pour cooked beans into a strainer and run water over them to cool.

6. When beans have cooled, combine all of the beans, celery, kalamata olives, red onion, parsley, dill, and lemon zest into a large bowl.

7. In a separate bowl, whisk together vinegar, sugar, vegetable oil, and Dijon mustard.

8. Add salt and pepper to taste.

9. Pour dressing over beans. Toss to coat. Refrigerate until ready to serve.

CILANTRO CHICKEN SALAD

Prep. Time: 30–45 minutes
Serves: 4

INGREDIENTS:

3 chicken breasts

1 cup chicken stock

2 heads iceberg lettuce, chopped

4 tomatoes, diced

2 cups chopped broccoli florets

1 bunch cilantro, chopped

¼ cup fresh lime juice

⅓ cup olive oil

½ tsp. cumin

¼ tsp. red pepper flakes

Salt and pepper to taste

DIRECTIONS:

1. Place steam basket into Instant Pot. Place chicken breasts onto steam rack.

2. Add 1 cup chicken stock. Secure lid as directed. Pressure cook on high for 15 minutes. Let the pressure release naturally.

3. While chicken is cooking, prepared salad greens in large bowl. Set aside.

4. To make dressing, add fresh lime juice, olive oil, cumin, red pepper flakes, salt, and pepper to a bowl. Combine well using whisk.

5. When chicken is fully cooked and pressure has released naturally from Instant Pot, remove chicken. Cut into bite-sized pieces.

6. If chicken is cold, add directly to salad. Pour dressing over salad. Toss to coat. If chicken is still hot, mix salad and dressing separately. Serve warm chicken on top of salad.

PASTA SALAD WITH CORN ON THE COB

Prep. Time: 45 minutes
Serves: 6–8

INGREDIENTS:

4 cups elbow macaroni

9 cups water, *divided*

2 cups chopped carrots

1 cup chopped asparagus

1 cup fresh or frozen peas

4 large eggs, hard-boiled
(see recipe on page 140)

2 tbsp. freshly chopped dill

⅓ cup chopped green
onions

¼ cup chopped chives

½ cup diced red bell pepper

1 tbsp. lemon zest

1 cup mayonnaise

1 tbsp. Dijon mustard

2 tsp. paprika

2 tsp. dried basil

Salt and pepper to taste

4 ears of corn

DIRECTIONS:

1. Add elbow macaroni, 8 cups water, carrots, asparagus, and peas to Instant Pot. Secure lid. Pressure cook on low for 5 minutes. Let steam release naturally.

2. Once steam has released, remove lid and strain pasta mixture under cold water until cool.

3. Peal and chop eggs, and place in a large bowl.

4. To the bowl, add the cooled macaroni, carrots, asparagus dill, green onions, chives, red bell pepper, lemon zest, mayonnaise, Dijon mustard, paprika, and basil. Gently fold together.

5. Salt and pepper to taste.

6. Place salad in refrigerator until ready to serve.

7. To cook corn on the cob, add corn to the Instant Pot along with 1 cup water. Secure lid and select steam mode. Adjust time for 5 minutes. When finished, allow steam to release naturally.

8. Carefully remove hot corn. Serve with butter, salt, pepper, and the chilled pasta salad.

POTATO SALAD

Prep. Time: 45 minutes
Serves: 6–8

INGREDIENTS:

5 russet potatoes

2 cups water, *divided*

3 carrots, peeled and diced

1 cup chopped broccoli

1 cup fresh or frozen peas

1 cup chopped celery

½ cup chopped green
    onions

1 cup freshly chopped Italian
    parsley

1 cup mayonnaise

Salt and freshly cracked
    pepper

DIRECTIONS:

1. Peel and cut potatoes into ½-inch dice.

2. Place potatoes inside Instant Pot. Add 1 cup water.

3. Secure lid and pressure cook on high for 5 minutes. Do a quick pressure release. Remove lid.

4. Strain potatoes and place in bowl of cold water to cool.

5. Place carrots and broccoli inside Instant Pot. Add 1 cup water. Secure lid.

6. Select steam mode and adjust time for 2 minutes. Do a quick pressure release. Remove lid.

7. Strain vegetables. Rinse under cold water to cool.

8. Place cooled potatoes, vegetables, parsley, and mayonnaise in a large bowl.

9. Gently fold together.

10. Add salt and pepper as needed.

11. Cover and place in refrigerator overnight before serving.

THE EVERYDAY INSTANT POT COOKBOOK

QUINOA AND ASIAN PEAR SALAD

Prep. Time: 45 minutes
Serves: 4–6

INGREDIENTS:

1 cup quinoa (rinsed, drained)

2⅓ cups water

2 Asian pears, cored, cut into ½-inch pieces

1 cup snow peas, chopped

1 red bell pepper, diced

¼ cup chopped pecans or walnuts, *optional*

4 green onions, chopped

¼ cup toasted sesame seeds

¼ cup fresh lemon juice

2 tbsp. olive oil

1 tsp. toasted sesame seed oil

Salt and pepper to taste

DIRECTIONS:

1. Rinse quinoa and place in the Instant Pot. Add 2⅓ cups water and secure lid.

2. Pressure cook on high for 10 minutes. Let pressure release naturally.

3. Meanwhile, using a large bowl, combine Asian pears, snow peas, bell pepper, pecans or walnuts (if using), green onions, sesame seeds, lemon juice, olive oil, and toasted sesame seed oil. Gently combine everything together and set aside.

4. When pressure has released, transfer quinoa to bowl containing other ingredients. Gently fold everything together and adjust salt and pepper as needed.

5. Chill salad for at least an hour before serving.

SALAMI AND PASTA SALAD

Prep. Time: 30 minutes
Serves: 6–8

INGREDIENTS:

4 cups elbow macaroni

8 cups water

4 large eggs, hard-boiled
(see recipe on page 140)

8 oz. salami, thinly sliced

1 small cucumber, peeled,
cut in half and sliced

2 cups chopped arugula

2 cups spinach

⅓ cup diced red onion

10 large stuffed green olives,
sliced in half

¼ cup extra-virgin olive oil

Salt and pepper to taste

1 lemon, cut into wedges

½ cup shredded Parmesan
cheese

DIRECTIONS:

1. Add elbow macaroni and 8 cups water to the
Instant Pot. Secure lid and pressure cook on low
for 8 minutes. Let steam release naturally.

2. Strain and rinse pasta until cool.

3. Peel and slice each egg in half and set aside.

4. Using a large bowl, add cooled macaroni, salami,
cucumber, arugula, spinach, red onion, and
sliced green olives.

5. Drizzle with ¼ cup extra-virgin olive oil; add salt
and pepper to taste. Gently mix together.

6. Divide between four dinner plates. Arrange hard-
boiled egg halves and lemon wedges on plates.
Sprinkle with Parmesan cheese.

SALMON NIÇOISE SALAD

Prep. Time: 45 minutes
Serves: 4

INGREDIENTS:

¾ cup extra-virgin olive oil

¼ cup rice vinegar

½ tsp. pepper

½ tsp. dry mustard

1 tsp. salt

2 tbsp. lemon juice

1 cup water

2 medium Klondike potatoes, diced (½-inch)

1 lb. green beans, snipped

4 eggs, hard-boiled (see recipe on page 140)

4 salmon fillets

1 bunch diced green onions

½ cup capers

4 tomatoes, chopped

12 black olives, pitted

1 tbsp. fresh chopped basil

DIRECTIONS:

1. To make the dressing: combine oil, vinegar, pepper, mustard, salt, and lemon juice. Whisk together and set aside.

2. Add steam rack to Instant Pot. Pour in 1 cup water. Add the potatoes, green beans, and salmon fillets, placing them on top of the steam rack. Be sure to arrange salmon fillets carefully so they are level.

3. Secure lid on the Instant Pot and pressure cook on low for 5 minutes. Allow pressure to release naturally.

4. Remove lid and carefully remove salmon fillets, potatoes, and green beans, and place salmon fillets onto a separate plate. Set aside.

5. Peel and set the eggs aside.

6. Combine potatoes, green beans, green onions, capers, tomatoes, olives, and basil in a large bowl.

7. Drizzle potato mixture with dressing and gently fold everything together. Make sure potatoes are well coated with dressing.

8. Divide potato mixture between four plates. Place a steamed salmon fillet on top of each plate. Slice each hard-boiled egg in half. Place an egg on each plate.

9. Serve the salad with your favorite bread.

SWEET POTATO QUINOA SALAD

Prep. Time: 30 minutes
Serves: 4–6

INGREDIENTS:

1 large sweet potato, peeled and diced into ½-inch pieces

1 cup quinoa, rinsed

2½ cups water

6–8 stalks celery, chopped

1 cup chopped artichoke hearts

1 cup chopped almonds

Juice from one large orange

¼ cup olive oil

Salt and pepper to taste

DIRECTIONS:

1. Add sweet potato pieces and quinoa to the Instant Pot. Pour in 2½ cups water. Secure Instant Pot lid.

2. Pressure cook on high for 5 minutes. Let pressure release naturally.

3. Carefully remove lid and strain off any excess water. Let sweet potatoes and quinoa cool completely.

4. In a large bowl, add sweet potatoes, quinoa, chopped celery, artichoke hearts, and almonds. Gently toss to combine everything together.

5. In a separate bowl, whisk the orange juice, olive oil, salt, and pepper together. Pour vinaigrette over the quinoa mixture.

6. Gently toss to combine.

7. Chill and serve.

THE EVERYDAY INSTANT POT COOKBOOK

WHITE BEAN SALAD WITH SKEWERED SHRIMP

Prep. Time: 45 minutes
Serves: 4

INGREDIENTS:

2 cups dry great northern beans

16 cups water, *divided*

24 shrimp, peeled and deveined

Salt and pepper to taste

2 Roma tomatoes, chopped

1 avocado, diced

½ cup freshly chopped parsley

¼ cup freshly chopped basil

2 tbsp. extra-virgin olive oil

1 tbsp. rice vinegar

DIRECTIONS:

1. Rinse uncooked beans. Be sure to pick out any little stones that may be present.

2. Add prepared beans to the Instant Pot along with 8 cups water. Let beans sit for 30 minutes to rehydrate. Drain beans and add another 8 cups clean water to them.

3. Secure lid on Instant Pot and pressure cook beans on high for 10 minutes. Allow pressure to release naturally. Test beans to make sure they are tender; if not, pressure cook for an additional 5 minutes.

4. Place six shrimp on each of four skewers (arrange so the shrimp lay flat on skewer).

5. Salt and pepper shrimp, then grill on both sides until fully cooked. Set aside until ready to use.

6. To make salad, drain and rinse cooked beans in cold water until cooled completely. Place in large bowl along with tomatoes, avocado, parsley, basil, extra-virgin olive oil, and rice vinegar. Gently toss everything together. Don't smash avocado.

7. Salt and pepper to taste.

8. Divide between four plates. Top with grilled shrimp skewers.

SOUPS

CHICKEN TORTELLINI SOUP

Prep. Time: 30 minutes
Serves: 4

INGREDIENTS:

6–8 cups chicken stock

1 onion, chopped

5 carrots, sliced

5 celery stalks, sliced

2 cups chopped kale

3 cups frozen green beans

4 cups chicken tortellini,
prepared per package
instructions

DIRECTIONS:

1. Pour chicken stock into Instant Pot. Add chopped onion, carrots, celery, kale, and green beans.

2. Secure lid and set Instant Pot to pressure cook on high for 3 minutes. Let pressure release naturally.

3. Remove lid and add the prepared chicken tortellini.

4. Place lid back on Instant Pot. Pressure cook on high for an additional 3 minutes. Quick-release the pressure. You may want to put a clean dish towel over the vent to prevent any liquid from splashing.

5. I like to serve this soup with freshly baked cinnamon rolls.

COUNTRY BEEF STEW

Prep. Time: 45 minutes
Serves: 6–8

INGREDIENTS:

Olive oil

1 large onion, sliced

6 garlic cloves

2 lb. stewing meat, cut into bite-sized pieces

2 quarts beef stock

1 can tomato paste

3 large potatoes, peeled and diced

4 small zucchini, chopped

4 small yellow squash, chopped

8 Roma tomatoes, chopped

1 green pepper, diced

1 red pepper, diced

1 yellow pepper, diced

6 celery stocks, chopped

4 large carrots, peeled and diced

¼ cup flour plus ½ cup beef stock mixed together

Salt and freshly cracked pepper to taste

DIRECTIONS:

1. Heat Instant Pot on Sauté mode. Add just enough olive oil to lightly coat bottom of the pot.

2. Add onion and garlic. Sauté for about 3 minutes.

3. Add stewing meat and brown.

4. Add beef stock along with all other ingredients.

5. Secure pressure cooker lid and pressure cook on high for 20 minutes.

6. Allow pressure to release naturally.

7. Serve with your favorite artisanal bread.

BUTTERNUT SQUASH SOUP

Prep. Time: 45 minutes
Serves: 4–6

INGREDIENTS:

4 cups cubed butternut
squash

1 large onion, sliced

6 garlic cloves, minced

1 turnip, chopped

2 carrots, dice

2 stalks celery, diced

Extra-virgin olive oil

6 cups chicken stock

2 cups heavy cream

Salt and pepper to taste

DIRECTIONS:

1. Add all ingredients into the Instant Pot and secure lid.

2. Pressure cook on high for 20 minutes.

3. Allow the pressure to release naturally. Remove lid.

4. Using an immersion blender, puree soup.

5. Serve with your favorite artisan bread.

BACON AND CORN CHOWDER

Prep. Time: 45 minutes
Serves: 6

INGREDIENTS:

½ lb. bacon, chopped up

1 medium onion, chopped

3 medium potatoes, peeled and diced (½-inch cubes)

4–5 stalks celery, chopped

3–4 carrots, peeled and chopped

3 cups corn

1 tbsp. paprika

2 tbsp. flour

2 cups milk

3 cups chicken stock

Salt and freshly cracked pepper to taste

½ cup freshly chopped parsley (garnish)

DIRECTIONS:

1. Set Instant Pot on Sauté mode and allow to heat up.

2. Add bacon and sauté for 2–3 minutes.

3. Add chopped onion and diced potatoes and sauté for another 2–3 minutes.

4. Add chopped celery, carrots, corn, and paprika to the bacon. Sauté for another minute.

5. Sprinkle bacon and vegetables with flour and stir to incorporate.

6. Once flour is incorporated, pour milk and chicken stock into pot. Stir to incorporate everything.

7. Secure the Instant Pot lid. Set the pressure cooker on low for 10 minutes. Let pressure release naturally.

8. Once pressure has released, remove lid, adjust salt and pepper to taste. Sprinkle with chopped parsley to garnish.

GARLIC TOMATO SOUP

Prep. Time: 45 minutes
Serves: 6–8

INGREDIENTS:

14 tomatoes, sliced in half

1 tbsp. minced garlic

1 large onion, chopped

2 bell peppers, chopped

6 cups chicken stock

2 cups cream

2 cups chopped fresh basil leaves

Salt and freshly cracked pepper to taste

Extra-virgin olive oil

DIRECTIONS:

1. Place tomatoes into the instant pot.

2. Add garlic, onion, bell peppers and chicken stock.

3. Secure Instant Pot lid. Pressure cook on high for 20 minutes.

4. Allow pressure to release naturally.

5. Once pressure has released, add cream and basil.

6. Using an immersion blender, puree ingredients together. Add salt and pepper to taste.

7. I like to drizzle extra-virgin olive oil over each bowl of soup before serving.

GREAT NORTHERN BEAN AND KLONDIKE ROSE POTATO SOUP

Prep. Time: 60 minutes
Serves: 6–8

INGREDIENTS:

1½ cups dry great northern beans

8 cups water

8 cups chicken stock

2 cups chopped kale

2 tbsp. Italian herb blend

4 medium Klondike Rose potatoes, cut into pieces

2 tbsp. tomato paste

1 tbsp. olive oil

2 cups chopped onions

1 cup chopped carrot

1 cup chopped celery

2 garlic cloves, minced

Salt and pepper to taste

4 cups spinach

DIRECTIONS:

1. Rinse great northern beans, checking to make sure there are no small stones.

2. Place beans inside Instant Pot. Add 8 cups water and let the beans rehydrate for 30 minutes.

3. Strain water off beans and pour chicken stock over them. Secure lid. Pressure cook on high for 20 minutes. Allow steam to release naturally.

4. Remove lid and add remaining ingredients *except* spinach.

5. Secure Instant Pot lid. Pressure cook on low for 5 minutes. Allow steam to release naturally.

6. Remove lid and stir in spinach. Let soup sit for 10 minutes before serving.

MAYAN LIME SOUP

Prep. Time: 45 minutes
Serves: 4–6

INGREDIENTS:

3 chicken breasts

4 cups chicken stock

3 tbsp. frying oil

1 garlic clove, crushed

1 small onion, sliced

1 fresh red pepper, sliced

2 ripe red tomatoes, chopped

2 bay leaves

2 limes, juiced and zest removed

Garnish:

½ lb. corn tortilla thin strips (fried to a golden crispy texture)

1 lime, thinly sliced

DIRECTIONS:

1. Place chicken breasts and chicken stock into Instant Pot. Pressure cook on high for 30 minutes. Let pressure release naturally.

2. When steam has released, remove lid and carefully shred chicken breasts. Add them back into stock.

3. Add crushed garlic clove, onion, red pepper, tomatoes, bay leaves, and zest and juice from 2 limes. Pressure cook on low for 3 minutes. Let pressure release naturally.

4. Remove lid and the bay leaves and ladle soup into favorite soup bowls.

5. Garnish each with fried corn tortilla strips and a thin slice of lime.

SPICY PORK RAMEN

Prep. Time: 45 minutes
Serves: 4

INGREDIENTS:

1 cup dry kidney beans

6 cups cold water

Vegetable oil

1½ lb. country-style pork ribs

6 cups chicken stock

1 can (16 oz.) diced tomatoes, with juice

1 tbsp. hot chili sauce

3 carrots, chopped

2 onions, chopped

5–6 garlic cloves, peeled and minced

4 bay leaves

1 tsp. dried oregano

2 cups corn

6 pkgs. ramen noodles

Salt and pepper to taste

Garnish:

1 bunch cilantro, chopped

1 bunch green onions chopped

1 Japanese fish cake (Narutomaki), sliced

2 cups diced extra firm tofu

3 hard-boiled eggs

DIRECTIONS:

1. Soak dry kidney beans in 6 cups cold water for 30 minutes. Drain water.

2. Select Sauté mode on Instant Pot. Add enough oil to lightly coat bottom of pan.

3. Add country-style pork ribs. Brown all sides.

4. Add chicken stock, tomatoes, chili sauce, kidney beans, carrots, onions, garlic, bay leaves, and oregano.

5. Pressure cook on high for 30 minutes. Allow steam to release naturally.

6. Remove lid. Make sure ribs shred easily and kidney beans are cooked. If not, pressure cook for 10 minutes longer, or adjust additional cooking time as needed. Allow pressure to release naturally.

7. Once cooked, select Sauté mode and add corn while bringing soup to a boil. Place ramen noodles in pot. Cook noodles for about 3 minutes or until tender. Add salt and pepper to taste.

8. Divide broth, pork, beans, and noodles between 4 large bowls, removing any bay leaves and garnishing with chopped cilantro, green onions, sliced fish cake, diced tofu, and hard-boiled eggs (see recipe on page 140).

SPLIT PEA AND HAM SOUP

Prep. Time: 45 minutes
Serves: 4–6

INGREDIENTS:

2 cups dry split peas

8 cups cold water

5–6 cups chicken stock

2 cups cubed ham

1 large onion, coarsely
    chopped

1 yam, peeled and diced

1 tsp. garlic powder

1 tsp. onion powder

1 tbsp. Italian seasoning herb
    blend

Salt and pepper to taste

Croutons and sour cream,
    for garnish

DIRECTIONS:

1. Wash spilt peas and remove any stones that may be present.

2. Soak split peas in 8 cups cold water for 30 minutes before using. Drain water.

3. Combine split peas, chicken stock, cubed ham, chopped onion, and diced yam in Instant Pot. Secure lid. Pressure cook on high for 10 minutes. Do a quick steam release to release pressure. (I like to place a kitchen towel over the steam release to catch any liquid that may come out.)

4. Once steam has been released, carefully remove lid. Add garlic and onion powder, Italian seasoning, and salt and pepper to taste.

5. Secure lid on Instant Pot. Pressure cook on high for 2 minutes. Allow steam to release naturally. Remove lid.

6. Serve soup with a dollop of sour cream and croutons.

UDON NOODLE SOUP WITH CHICKEN, CABBAGE, AND SCALLIONS

Prep. Time: 45 minutes
Serves: 4

INGREDIENTS:

Udon Noodles:

2½ cups flour

½ cup tapioca starch

1 tsp. salt

Soup Base:

4 cups water

½ cup miso soup base

2 tbsp. bonito soup stock

1 tsp. red pepper flakes

1 tbsp. minced ginger

¼ cup soy sauce

2 tbsp. mirin

2 chicken breasts

Toppings:

Shredded cabbage

Chopped green onions

DIRECTIONS:

1. To make noodles, combine flour, tapioca starch, salt, and 1 cup water in the bowl of your stand mixer. Using the paddle attachment, mix the dough until smooth (about 5 minutes). When using the paddle attachment, watch machine carefully as it may bump around a lot.

2. Once noodle dough is ready, remove from machine. Divide into 2 parts. Roll dough onto a floured work surface, forming a rectangle ¼-inch thick. Dust dough well with flour. Fold into thirds lengthwise.

3. Slice noodles as wide as you like. I like mine ⅛ inch.

4. Toss noodles with flour to prevent them from sticking. Set aside until ready to use.

5. To the Instant Pot, add 4 cups water, miso soup base, bonito soup stock, red pepper flakes, minced ginger, soy sauce, mirin, and chicken breasts. Secure lid and pressure cook on high for 10 minutes. Let steam release naturally.

6. Remove lid and chicken breasts. Carefully slice the chicken breasts and set aside. Add prepared noodles to soup and gently stir to combine.

7. Secure lid back on Instant Pot. Select Steam mode and steam for 3 minutes. Let steam release naturally.

8. Remove Instant Pot lid.

9. Ladle soup into 4 bowls. Arrange sliced chicken breasts, shredded cabbage, and chopped scallions on top of each bowl.

VEGETABLE KALE SOUP

Prep. Time: 45 minutes
Serves: 6–8

INGREDIENTS:

Extra-virgin olive oil

6 Klondike potatoes, cut into 1-inch pieces

2 medium carrots, sliced into rounds

2 celery ribs, sliced

1 medium onion, coarsely chopped

1 cup barley

1 lb. fresh green beans, snipped and cut into 1-inch lengths

8 cups vegetable stock

2 tbsp. freshly chopped parsley

1 tbsp. freshly chopped tarragon

1 bunch kale, chopped

Salt and pepper to taste

DIRECTIONS:

1. Heat Instant Pot on Sauté mode. Add enough extra-virgin olive oil to lightly coat bottom of the pot.

2. Add Klondike potatoes, carrots, celery, onion, barley, and green beans to pot. Sauté for 5 minutes.

3. Add remaining ingredients and secure lid.

4. Pressure cook on low for 20 minutes. Allow steam to release naturally.

WHITE BEAN AND KALE SOUP

Prep. Time: 60 minutes
Serves: 6–8

INGREDIENTS:

1½ cups dry white beans

8 cups cold water

8 cups chicken stock

2 cups chopped kale

2 tsp. chopped fresh thyme

1 tsp. fennel seeds, crushed
(If you don't have a mortar and pestle to crush the fennel seeds, roll your rolling pin over them to crush them.)

½ tsp. dried marjoram

2 tbsp. tomato paste

1 tbsp. olive oil

2 cups chopped onions

1 cup chopped carrot

1 cup chopped celery

2 garlic cloves, minced

½ tsp. freshly ground black pepper

¼ tsp. salt

Garnish, *optional:*

2 tbsp. diced red bell pepper

2 tbsp. chopped fresh basil

2 tbsp. finely chopped green onions

DIRECTIONS:

1. Wash beans. Make sure there are no stones in them.

2. Soak beans in 8 cups cold water for 30 minutes. Drain off water.

3. Place beans in the Instant Pot along with 8 cups chicken stock. Secure lid. Pressure cook on high for 30 minutes. Allow steam to release naturally.

4. Remove lid from pressure cooker. Add remaining ingredients.

5. Secure Instant Pot lid back on. Pressure cook on low for 5 minutes. Allow steam to release naturally.

6. Serve with your favorite garnishes, like the ones listed, if desired.

MEAT ENTRÉES

PORK ROAST

Prep. Time: 2½ hours
Serves: 6–8

INGREDIENTS:

4–6-lb. boneless pork roast

Kitchen twine

Olive oil

1½ cups vegetable stock

6 cups chopped root
  vegetables (your choice)

Herb Rub 1:

¼ cup freshly chopped
  rosemary

2 tbsp. freshly chopped
  thyme

¼ cup chopped dried
  apricots

Zest of 1 orange

1 tsp. cinnamon

1 tbsp. onion powder

1 tbsp. freshly cracked
  pepper

2 tsp. salt

¼ cup extra-virgin olive oil

Herb Rub 2:

1 tbsp. smoked paprika

1 tbsp. onion powder

1 tbsp. garlic powder

1 tbsp. freshly cracked
  pepper

1 tsp. salt

2 tbsp. extra-virgin olive oil

DIRECTIONS:

1. Being very careful not to cut all the way through the pork roast, slice roast down the center, cutting about ¾ of the way through. Unfold the roast so it lays open. Then, repeating the previous step, slice ¾ of the way through each of the halves so that the meat lays flat. There should now be three cuts in the meat. Set aside.

2. Combine Herb Rub 1 ingredients in a medium bowl. Mix until combined.

3. Rub herb mixture on inside portion of roast. Tie roast back together and set aside.

4. Combine Herb Rub 2 ingredients in a small bowl. Mix together until combined.

5. Distribute Herb Rub 2 over the outside of the pork roast.

6. Place steam rack into Instant Pot. Add vegetable stock.

7. Place prepared roast onto steam rack. Pressure cook on high for 90 minutes.

8. Allow steam to release naturally. Remove lid. Check to make sure roast is tender and easily shredded. If needed, pressure cook the roast on high for an additional 15 minutes. When finished, allow steam to release naturally.

9. Add root vegetables to Instant Pot. Set pressure to low and cook for 3 minutes. Allow pressure to release naturally.

10. Remove vegetables and pork roast. Slice or shred roast and serve with the freshly cooked root vegetables and drippings.

11. If desired, make a pork gravy (recipe found in Country Pork Ribs recipe, page 79). Serve with mashed potatoes, if desired.

COUNTRY PORK RIBS

Prep. Time: 90 minutes
Serves: 6–8

INGREDIENTS:

3–4 lb. country-style pork ribs

2 cups prepared barbecue sauce

2 cups chicken stock

1 cup apricot jam

1 tbsp. smoked paprika

1 tbsp. garlic powder

1 tbsp. onion powder

1 tbsp. chili powder

1 tbsp. herbes de Provence

Salt and freshly cracked pepper to taste

Pork Gravy:

⅓ cup flour

Pork drippings

DIRECTIONS:

1. Place country-style pork ribs into the Instant Pot. (Country-style pork ribs are boneless pork ribs.)

2. Add the barbecue sauce, chicken stock, apricot jam, smoked paprika, garlic powder, onion powder, chili powder, and herbes de Provence.

3. Gently stir everything together. Secure lid onto the Instant Pot.

4. Pressure cook on high for 45 minutes. Allow pressure to release naturally.

5. Use pork drippings to make a pork gravy:

   1. Make a flour slurry by combining flour and ½ cup water together. Pour into pork dripping.

   2. Bring drippings to a boil until they thicken. Strain gravy if needed. Adjust seasonings to taste and enjoy. Serve with Delicious Mashed Potatoes (page 3).

THE EVERYDAY INSTANT POT COOKBOOK

CHICKEN AND DUMPLINGS

Prep. Time: 60 minutes
Serves: 4–6

INGREDIENTS:

4 tbsp. butter

Extra-virgin olive oil

2 chicken breasts, cut into bite-sized pieces

1 large onion, minced

2 garlic cloves, minced

2 cups sliced mushrooms

10-oz. pkg. frozen peas and carrots

¼ cup flour

2 cups milk

4 cups chicken stock

1 tbsp. dried sage

Salt and pepper to taste

Dumplings:

2 cups all-purpose flour

1 tbsp. baking powder

1 tbsp. sugar

1½ tsp. salt

⅓ cup lard, shortening, or butter

½ cup milk (plus more if needed)

1 egg

1 tbsp. freshly chopped chives

½ tsp. black pepper

DIRECTIONS:

1. Heat Instant Pot on Sauté mode. Add butter and drizzle enough olive oil to lightly coat bottom of pot.

2. Add chopped chicken breasts, onion, garlic, and mushrooms to the Instant Pot. Sauté chicken mixture for 5 minutes. When you start to see color on the chicken pieces, add frozen peas and carrots.

3. Sprinkle flour over top of chicken mixture. Gently stir to incorporate flour into oil.

4. Add milk, chicken stock, sage, and salt and pepper (to taste), stirring everything together to combine. Stir and secure Instant Pot lid. Pressure cook on high for 15 minutes.

5. To make the dumplings, combine all-purpose flour, baking powder, sugar, and 1 teaspoon of the salt into a large mixing bowl and mix together. Next, cut cold lard, shortening, or butter into dry ingredients until it resembles cornmeal. (I like to do this in my food processor with the blade attachment and pulse it a few times until the fat has been cut into dry ingredients.)

6. Then mix in milk, egg, chives, remaining salt, and black pepper and set aside until needed.

7. When pressure cooker is finished, quick release pressure and remove lid.

8. Spoon dumpling mixture on top of soup one spoonful at a time.

9. Place lid back onto pressure cooker and secure in place. Change Instant Pot setting to Steam. Let steam for 10 minutes. Let pressure release naturally.

THE EVERYDAY INSTANT POT COOKBOOK

EASY POT ROAST

Prep. Time: 2½ hours
Serves: 6–8

INGREDIENTS:

Olive oil

6-lb. beef roast

10 garlic cloves

1 medium onion

½ cup fresh rosemary

¼ cup fresh thyme

¼ cup extra-virgin olive oil

2 tbsp. balsamic vinegar

2 tbsp. Worcestershire sauce

2 cups beef stock

2 tbsp. freshly cracked
    pepper

Salt to taste

6 cups root vegetables
    peeled (if needed) and
    cut into ½-inch and
    ¾-inch thick pieces

Roux:

2 tbsp. butter

2 tbsp. flour

DIRECTIONS:

1. Select Sauté mode and heat Instant Pot. Add enough olive oil to lightly coat bottom of pot. Brown roast on all sides.

2. Add remaining ingredients *except* root vegetables, into pressure cooker. Secure lid.

3. Pressure cook on high for 90 minutes.

4. Let steam release naturally. If needed, pressure cook and additional 15 minutes.

5. When roast is tender, add root vegetables and secure lid again. Set pressure cooker to steam mode and steam for 3 minutes. Let pressure release naturally.

6. When roast is finished, strain juices and thicken them with a roux to create a gravy, if desired.

7. To make the roux:
   - In a sauté pan, add 2 tbsp. of butter on medium heat, gently melting the butter.
   - Once the butter has melted, stir in 2 tbsp. of flour until blended. Remove from the heat, set aside until ready to use.

8. Serve the easy pot roast with root vegetables, fresh bread, and Country-Style Potatoes (page 2).

HAWAIIAN STYLE KALÚA PORK AND RICE

Prep. Time: 2 hours
Serves: 6–8

INGREDIENTS:

4-lb. pork shoulder roast

1 tbsp. sea salt

1 tsp. liquid smoke

6 cups vegetable stock

4 cups rice

1 cup water

DIRECTIONS:

1. Cut pork shoulder roast in half and sprinkle with sea salt. Set aside.

2. Add liquid smoke (be careful because a little goes a long way) and vegetable stock to Instant Pot.

3. Place steam rack into pot and place pork shoulder roast on top of steam rack.

4. Secure lid and pressure cook on high for 90 minutes. Let pressure release naturally.

5. Using two forks, check pork shoulder roast for tenderness. If you can't easily shred it, secure Instant Pot lid again and pressure cook on high for an additional 15 minutes. Repeat as needed.

6. When roast is easy to shred, transfer entire roast and liquid to large bowl and set aside.

7. Add 4 cups rice to Instant Pot bowl. Add 4 cups of the liquid from pork roast and 1 cup water to rice.

8. Secure lid. Use Rice mode on the Instant Pot to cook rice.

9. If you don't have a Rice mode, pressure cook rice for 8 minutes on low pressure. Let the steam release naturally. Remove lid when steam has released.

10. While rice is cooking, shred pork.

11. I like to serve the shredded pork and rice with green beans, freshly sliced pineapple, and Hawaiian rolls on the side.

THE EVERYDAY INSTANT POT COOKBOOK

SHREDDED PORK TOSTADAS WITH MASHED POTATOES

Prep. Time: 90 minutes
Serves: 6

INGREDIENTS:

2-lb. pork shoulder roast

2 cups vegetable stock

Salt and pepper to taste

3 large russet potatoes, peeled and cut into pieces

1 cup sharp shredded cheese

12 tostada shells

1 red bell pepper, diced

1 bunch green onions, chopped

2 cups shredded lettuce

1 cup diced tomatoes

Hot sauce

DIRECTIONS:

1. To make shredded pork, cut pork roast into 4 equal parts and place in Instant Pot. Pour vegetable stock over it and sprinkle with salt and pepper.

2. Secure Instant Pot lid. Pressure cook on high for 90 minutes. Let pressure release naturally.

3. Remove lid and shred pork with a couple of forks. If needed, you can adjust cooking times longer to make sure pork shreds easily.

4. Remove pork and place potatoes into the drippings of the pork roast.

5. Place lid back on the Instant Pot and pressure cook on high for 5 minutes. Let the steam release naturally when finished.

6. Remove potatoes using a slotted spoon or strainer.

7. Place potatoes into a large bowl along with shredded cheese. Mash together. Adjust salt and pepper to taste.

8. To assemble tostadas, place a dollop of mashed potatoes followed by some shredded pork, sprinkling of diced red bell pepper, green onions, shredded lettuce, and diced tomatoes on top of a prepared tostada shell. Serve with your favorite hot sauce.

BBQ CHICKEN TENDERS

Prep. Time: 45 minutes
Serves: 4–6

INGREDIENTS:

1 cup sugar

1 stick (8 tbsp.) butter, melted

½ cup corn syrup

½ cup water

1 cup diced onion

4 garlic gloves, minced

2 cups prepared barbecue
  sauce

15 chicken tenders

DIRECTIONS:

1. Add the sugar, butter, corn syrup, ½ cup water, onion, garlic, and barbecue sauce to the Instant Pot. Stir everything together.

2. Pressure cook on high for 10 minutes, letting the steam release naturally.

3. When the steam has released, transfer the sauce to a bowl and add the chicken tenders to the Instant Pot with 1 cup water. Secure the lid and pressure cook on high for 5 minutes, letting the pressure release naturally.

4. When the steam has released, remove the lid and transfer the chicken tenders to a large bowl. Sprinkle with 1 tbsp. of the spice rub (recipe below) and toss to coat.

5. Drizzle the chicken tenders with the sauce, toss, and serve with your favorite vegetables and enjoy!

SPICE RUB FOR CHICKEN TENDERS

2 tbsp. dried parsley

2 tsp. dried dill

1 tbsp. onion powder

1 tbsp. garlic powder

1 tsp. paprika

¼ tsp. cayenne pepper

2 tsp. salt

2 tsp. pepper

Combine all of the ingredients in a small bowl and mix together. Use as needed.

BEEF SAUERBRATEN

Prep. Time: 2½ hours
Serves: 6–8

INGREDIENTS:

1 cup red wine vinegar

1 cup water

1 large onion, chopped

5 whole cloves

1 tbsp. dry dill

¼ cup sugar

1 tbsp. ground pepper

2 tsp. salt

3–4-lb. beef roast

DIRECTIONS:

1. Add red wine vinegar, 1 cup water, onion, cloves, dill, sugar, pepper, and salt to the Instant Pot.

2. Set Instant Pot on Sauté and bring mixture to a boil. Stir to dissolve sugar and salt.

3. Place the steam rack into the Instant Pot and the beef roast on top. Secure lid and pressure cook on high for 2 hours.

4. Let pressure release naturally. Remove lid when safe. Check roast for tenderness. Serve with red cabbage, Country-Style Potatoes (page 2), and freshly baked rolls.

BEEF STROGANOFF

Prep. Time: 45 minutes
Serves: 6–8

INGREDIENTS:

Extra-virgin olive oil

1 lb. beef chuck roast, cut into bite-sized cubes

1 medium mushroom

3 garlic cloves, minced

3 cups beef stock

2 tsp. thyme

1 bay leaf

1 pkg. egg noodles (I like the wide ribbon ones)

¼ cup sour cream

1 tbsp. Dijon mustard

Salt and freshly cracked pepper

DIRECTIONS:

1. Heat Instant Pot on Sauté mode. Add just enough olive oil to lightly coat bottom of pot.

2. Add meat, butter, onions, mushrooms, and garlic. Sauté for 5 minutes.

3. Add beef stock to deglaze pan.

4. Add thyme and bay leaf.

5. Secure lid on Instant Pot. Pressure cook on high for 15 minutes.

6. While beef and vegetable mixture is cooking, follow package directions for cooking egg noodles.

7. Once beef, vegetable, and herb mixture has finished cooking, let the pressure release naturally.

8. Once the pressure has released, stir in the sour cream and Dijon mustard. Remove bay leaf before serving. Salt and pepper to taste. Serve over prepared egg noodles.

CABBAGE ROLLS

Prep. Time: 45 minutes
Serves: 6–8

INGREDIENTS:

1 cup water

1 head cabbage

1 cup finely diced carrots

½ cup finely diced onion

½ cup finely diced green onions

2–3 lb. ground beef

1 tbsp. steak seasoning blend

1 tbsp. Worcestershire sauce

1 tbsp. minced garlic

2 cups instant rice

Sauce:

2 cans (14.5 oz) crushed tomatoes

1 can Italian style tomato paste

1 tbsp. Italian seasoning herb blend

1 cup water

DIRECTIONS:

1. Pour 1 cup water into Instant Pot and place the steam rack in the pot. Remove core from cabbage and place on steam rack.

2. Steam cook for 5 minutes. Let pressure release naturally.

3. When cabbage is cool enough to handle, remove leaves and set aside.

4. Add carrots, onion, and green onions to a food processor and finely pulse them together.

5. Add carrot mixture to a large bowl along with remaining ingredients (minus cabbage). Mix everything together.

6. Divide meat mixture between prepared cabbage leaves and fold cabbage leaves up like a burrito. Place on steam rack inside Instant Pot.

7. In a separate bowl mix the crushed tomatoes, tomato paste, Italian seasoning, and 1 cup water. Pour over the cabbage rolls.

8. Secure lid and pressure cook on high for 8 minutes. Let steam release naturally. Serve with your favorite sides.

CHOCOLATE CHILI

Prep. time: 45 minutes
Serves: 10–12

INGREDIENTS:

Olive oil

2 lb. extra-lean ground beef

2 large onions, diced

6 garlic cloves, minced

2 red bell peppers, diced

2 large (approx 32-oz.) cans
   kidney beans

2 large cans diced tomatoes

2 cups of beef broth

1 6-oz. can Italian-style
   tomato paste

2 tbsp. cumin

¼ cup cocoa powder

2 tsp. cinnamon

A few splashes of hot sauce

Salt and pepper to taste

DIRECTIONS:

1. Select the Sauté mode on the Instant Pot and let it heat up. Add enough olive oil to lightly coat bottom of the pot.

2. Add beef, onions, garlic, and bell peppers. Sauté for 5 minutes.

3. Add remaining ingredients (be sure to add juice from beans and the diced tomatoes) to pot and stir to incorporate. Secure lid and pressure cook on high for 15 minutes

4. Allow pressure to release naturally and remove the lid. Stir and serve with your favorite sides.

CORNED BEEF, CABBAGE, AND POTATOES

Prep. Time: 2 hours
Serves: 6–8

INGREDIENTS:

3–4 lb. corned beef brisket

2 bay leaves

1 tbsp black peppercorns

4 whole cloves

4 cloves garlic, smashed

1 tsp whole allspice berries

1 tbsp mustard seed

2 cups water

1 head green cabbage, cut into 6 wedges, core removed

1 pkg. Klondike Gourmet Medley Potatoes

DIRECTIONS:

1. Place steam rack into Instant Pot. Place corned beef on steam rack. Add 2 cups water and sprinkle corned beef with the spices. Pressure cook on high for 90 minutes, allowing pressure to release naturally.

2. Remove lid once pressure has released. Add cabbage and potatoes to the pot and pressure cook on high for an additional 5 minutes. Let pressure release naturally.

3. Serve with your favorite soda bread.

4. Remove the bay leaves before serving.

KIMCHI PORK DIM SUM

Prep. Time: 30 minutes
Serves: 6–8

INGREDIENTS:

1 lb. ground pork

1 cup chopped kimchi

1 tsp. ginger

1 tsp. granulated garlic

2 tbsp. soy sauce

2 tbsp. brown sugar

¼ cup freshly chopped chives

½ cup finely chopped onion

1 egg

1 cup + 1 tbsp. water, *divided*

egg roll wrappers

cooking oil

Dipping sauce:

¼ cup soy sauce

2 tsp. toasted sesame seed oil

¼ cup chopped chives

1 tbsp. brown sugar

½ tsp. red pepper flakes

DIRECTIONS:

1. In a large bowl, add pork, kimchi, ginger, garlic, soy sauce, brown sugar, chives, and onion. Mix everything together to combine.

2. Whisk egg with a tablespoon of water in a small bowl and set aside. Place an egg roll wrapper on a flat working surface and lightly brush the edges with egg wash.

3. Spoon 2–3 tablespoons of kimchi-pork filling onto center of egg wrapper. Fold each egg roll wrapper in half, pressing down to seal edges.

4. Gently press bottom of dim sum onto flat surface to create a flat bottom.

5. When ready, place steam rack in bottom of Instant Pot. Add 1 cup water. Spray bamboo steamer basket with vegetable spray and place it down onto the steam rack. (I use a round, stackable bamboo steamer that fits into the Instant Pot.)

6. Secure lid of Instant Pot and steam for 8 minutes, letting steam release naturally.

7. Transfer dim sum to a serving dish.

8. To make dipping sauce, add ingredients to a small bowl, whisking everything together. Serve dipping sauce with kimchi pork dim sum.

LEMON CAPER CHICKEN WITH EGG NOODLES

Prep. Time: 30 minutes
Serves: 4

INGREDIENTS:

2 lb. egg noodles

2 tbsp. freshly chopped rosemary

¼ freshly chopped basil

2 cups white wine

2 cups chicken stock

2 tbsp. freshly squeezed lemon juice

5 tbsp. cold butter, cut into tbsp. pieces

2 chicken breasts, flattened to ¼ inch thick

½ cup capers

Salt and ground pepper to taste

Red bell pepper, *optional*

Lemon slice, *optional*

DIRECTIONS:

1. Place egg noodles, rosemary, basil, white wine, chicken stock, and lemon juice into the Instant Pot.

2. Secure lid and pressure cook on high for 2 minutes. Allow steam to release naturally.

3. When steam has released, remove lid and gently stir in butter 1 tablespoon at a time.

4. Place chicken breasts on top of egg noodles and sprinkle with capers, and salt and pepper to taste. Secure lid and steam cook for 8 minutes allowing steam to release naturally.

5. Remove chicken breast and set aside.

6. Divide egg noodles and sauce between four pasta plates.

7. Cut chicken breasts into 4 portions. Serve on top with a sprinkle of freshly chopped red bell pepper and a lemon slice, if desired.

PORK TAMALES

Prep. Time: 2½ hours
Serves: 6–8

INGREDIENTS:

Olive oil

3-lb. bone-in pork roast

1 tsp. salt

1 tsp. black pepper

5 cups vegetable stock

1 pkg. dried corn husks

½ cup lard

4 cups Maseca corn flour

1 cup frozen corn

⅓ cup chopped green chilies

1 cup water

DIRECTIONS:

1. Heat Instant Pot on Sauté mode. Add enough oil to lightly coat bottom of pot.

2. Place pork roast into the pot. Sprinkle with salt and pepper. Brown all sides of roast.

3. Pour vegetable stock over roast. Secure Instant Pot lid.

4. Pressure cook on high for 90 minutes. Let steam release naturally. Reserve the pork drippings to make the masa in step 8.

5. While roast is cooking, place dried corn husks in a large bowl of water. Weigh them down so they rehydrate and become pliable (about 30 minutes).

6. When roast is cooked, shred with a couple of forks.

7. To make masa, cream lard until light and fluffy using mixer with paddle attachment. Add Maseca corn flour, frozen corn, and green chilies. Mix everything together.

8. Add 1–2 cups of the pork roast drippings, mixing until a soft dough is formed.

9. Place a generous portion of prepared masa onto the upper center of wide end of corn husk. Place a large piece of shredded pork over masa. Fold sides over and bring bottom portion of husk up over the masa. Repeat to make about a dozen tamales, depending on their size.

10. Place steam rack into Instant Pot and place the tamales open end up on top of the steam rack. You should have enough tamales to support each other upright in pot. Pour 1 cup water into bottom of pot. Secure lid.

11. Pressure cook on low for 30 minutes. Let steam release naturally. Remove lid.

12. Gently remove tamales. Serve with your favorite salsa on the side.

COUNTRY RIBS

Prep. Time: 1 hour
Serves: 6–8

INGREDIENTS:

Extra-virgin olive oil

6 pork boneless country spare ribs

2 cups pale ale

3 tbsp. pepper jelly

3 tbsp. apple jelly

1 tbsp. Dijon mustard

1 tbsp. herbes de Provence

1 tbsp. beef bouillon

2 tsp. seasoned salt

1 tbsp. black pepper

1 tsp. cumin

2 tbsp. Worcestershire sauce

2 tbsp. soy sauce

2 tbsp. cornstarch

DIRECTIONS:

1. Preheat Instant Pot on Sauté mode. Add enough extra-virgin olive oil to lightly coat bottom of pot.

2. Add pork spare ribs into Instant Pot, browning all sides.

3. In a mixing bowl, add pale ale, pepper jelly, apple jelly, Dijon mustard, herbes de Provence, beef bouillon, seasoned salt, black pepper, cumin, Worcestershire sauce, soy sauce, and cornstarch. Whisk together to combine.

4. Pour mixture over ribs in the Instant Pot.

5. Secure lid on the Instant Pot and pressure cook on high for 45 minutes. Allow pressure to release naturally.

6. Remove lid and, using a fork, check tenderness of the pork ribs. If needed, pressure cook an additional 10 minutes or until desired tenderness is reached.

7. Serve ribs with your favorite side dishes.

SPICY BEEF TAMALES

Prep. Time: 2½ hours
Serves: 6–8

INGREDIENTS:

Olive oil

3-lb. beef roast

1 tsp. salt

1 tsp. black pepper

1 cup spicy salsa

5 cups beef stock

1 pkg. corn husks

½ cup lard

4 cups Maseca corn flour

1 cup water

1 cup prepared tomatillo
    salsa

DIRECTIONS:

1. Add enough olive oil to lightly coat bottom of Instant Pot. Select Sauté mode and let pot heat.

2. Place beef roast in Instant Pot. Sprinkle with salt and pepper. Brown all sides of the roast.

3. Pour spicy salsa and beef stock over roast. Secure Instant Pot lid as directed.

4. Pressure cook on high for 90 minutes. Allow pressure to naturally release. Reserve drippings.

5. While roast is cooking, place dried corn husks in a large bowl of warm water. Use a heavy object to press them down into the water for about 30 minutes. Unless corn husks are rehydrated, they won't wrap around tamale dough.

6. Make masa: In a large mixer using the paddle attachment, cream lard until light and fluffy. Add the Maseca corn flour and prepared tomatillo salsa along with 1 cup of the beef roast drippings to the mixture. Mix thoroughly. If needed, add additional beef stock to pull mixture into a soft dough.

7. When beef roast has cooled, shred it.

8. To assemble tamales, place a rehydrated corn husk in front of you, pointed end facing you. Place a good portion of prepared masa in upper center of wide end of the corn husk. Place a large piece of shredded beef over masa. Fold sides over

and lift bottom portion of husk up over masa. Repeat to make about a dozen more tamales, depending on their size.

9. Place steam rack in Instant Pot. Pour 1 cup water into pot. Place tamales open-side up into pot. You should have enough tamales so that they hold each other upright in pot.

10. Pressure cook on high for 20 minutes. Let pressure release naturally.

11. Once pressure has released, carefully remove lid and lift tamales from pot.

12. Serve with your favorite salsa.

SLOPPY JOES

Prep. Time: 45 minutes
Serves: 6–8

INGREDIENTS:

1 lb. ground beef

1 large onion, chopped

1 bell pepper, chopped

1 tbsp. garlic powder

1 tsp. dry mustard

1 tbsp. dried dill

1 tbsp. dried parsley

¼ cup dried buttermilk powder

1 tbsp. brown sugar

1 cup ketchup

6-oz. can tomato paste

2 cups water

Salt and pepper to taste

Hamburger buns

DIRECTIONS:

1. Add ingredients (expect hamburger buns) to the Instant Pot.

2. Stir mixture to combine and secure the lid. Pressure cook on low for 30 minutes. Allow steam to release naturally.

3. Remove lid and gently stir.

4. When Sloppy Joe mixture is cooked, spoon onto hamburger buns.

5. Serve with fresh coleslaw and chips.

STEAK FAJITAS

Prep. Time: 30 minutes
Serves: 6–8

INGREDIENTS:

1-lb. New York strip steak

2 tbsp. Worcestershire sauce

1 tsp. freshly diced garlic

1 green bell pepper

1 red bell pepper

1 yellow bell pepper

1 medium onion

Olive oil

2 garlic cloves, minced

½ cup water

1 cup thinly sliced green
    cabbage

½ cup chopped cilantro

juice and zest from 1 lime

¼ cup golden raisins

Salt and pepper to taste

Flour tortillas

Spice Mix:

½ tsp. seasoned salt

1 tsp. pepper

½ tsp. garlic powder

½ tsp. onion powder

½ tsp. cumin

½ tsp. cayenne pepper

DIRECTIONS:

1. Cut New York strip steak into thin slices. Place in large bowl. Add Worcestershire sauce and diced garlic; mix together and marinate for 15 minutes.

2. While steak is marinating, clean and slice bell peppers and onion into thin, lengthwise cuts. In a small bowl, whisk the ingredients for the spice mix (bottom of the ingredient list) together and set aside until ready to use.

3. Heat Instant Pot on Sauté mode. Add enough olive oil to lightly coat bottom of pot. When hot, remove New York strip steak from marinade and sauté for about 1 minute.

4. Add sliced bell peppers, onion, garlic, spice mix, and ½ cup water and ⅓ cup of the marinade.

5. Secure lid and select Steam mode. Steam for 5 minutes. When finished, do a quick release.

6. Remove lid and fold in cabbage, cilantro, lime juice and zest, and raisins. Add salt and pepper to taste.

7. Place fajita mixture on a large platter accompanied by flour tortillas and freshly quartered limes.

STEAMED PORK BUNS

Prep. Time: 2 hours
Serves: 6–8

INGREDIENTS:

Dough:

2 tsp. instant yeast

¼ cup honey

⅓ cup powdered milk

2 tsp. baking powder

2 cups lukewarm water
    (about 105°F)

1 stick (8 tbsp.) butter, melted

2 tsp. salt

5–6 cups bread flour, plus
    more if necessary

Filling:

4 cups cooked pork roast
    (use Pork Roast recipe,
    page 76)

1 cup water

Condiments:

Hoisin sauce

DIRECTIONS:

1. In your stand mixer's bowl, using the paddle attachment, combine yeast, honey, powdered milk, baking powder, and water. Stir to blend.

2. Let stand until foamy, about 5 minutes. Mix in melted butter and salt.

3. Change paddle attachment to dough hook. Add flour, a little at a time, mixing at lowest speed until most of flour has been absorbed, and a soft dough forms.

4. Continue mixing/kneading dough for 5 minutes. Dust the dough with flour, if necessary, to keep dough from sticking.

5. Place dough in a greased bowl. Spray top with vegetable oil to prevent dough from drying out while proofing. Loosely cover dough. Let double in size.

6. To assemble pork buns, divide dough into ten pieces just larger than a golf ball.

7. Roll out and flatten each piece of dough into a round circle about a quarter of an inch thick.

8. Place a portion of the pulled pork in the center and gather edges up around filling.

9. Using your thumb and index finger, pinch top and slightly twist it clockwise about 30 degrees to add a decorative twist to bun.

10. Place each pork bun on a square piece of parchment paper about 2 inches x 2 inches or just large enough to hold the pork bun.

11. Pour 1 cup water into the Instant Pot. Place prepared pork buns onto a bamboo steamer. Place into the Instant Pot. Bamboo steamers come in many sizes, so choose one that easily fits inside your Instant Pot.

12. Select Steam mode on Instant Pot and steam for 10 minutes. Use a quick steam release to release the steam.

13. Serve steamed pork buns with hoisin sauce.

THE EVERYDAY INSTANT POT COOKBOOK

SWEET-AND-SOUR CHICKEN OVER RICE

Prep. Time: 45 minutes
Serves: 6–8

INGREDIENTS:

Olive oil

4 chicken breasts, cut into 1-inch pieces

1 cup chicken stock

2 large onions, sliced

1 bell pepper, cut into 1-inch pieces

1 bunch green onions, sliced

8-oz. can pineapple chunks, drained (reserve juice)

¾ cup sugar

½ cup red wine vinegar

2 tbsp. cornstarch (mix with reserved pineapple juice)

Salt and pepper to taste

DIRECTIONS:

1. Select Sauté mode on the Instant Pot. Add just enough olive oil to lightly coat bottom of the pot.

2. Add the chicken pieces to the pot and sauté for 2 minutes, or until they have a little color on them.

3. Pour chicken stock into the Instant Pot and secure the lid. Pressure cook on high for 10 minutes. Use a quick steam release to release the pressure.

4. Once steam is released, remove lid. Add onion slices, bell pepper, green onions, pineapple chunks, sugar, red wine vinegar, and the cornstarch/pineapple juice mixture. Stir to incorporate everything.

5. Pressure cook on low for 5 minutes and use a quick-release method to release the pressure.

6. Season with salt and pepper to taste. Serve sweet-and-sour chicken mixture over rice. Use the Basic White Rice (page 13) or Basic Brown Rice recipe (page 11).

PASTA

THE EVERYDAY INSTANT POT COOKBOOK

ONE-POT SPAGHETTI

Prep. Time: 30 minutes
Serves: 6–8

INGREDIENTS:

1 lb. spaghetti

24-oz. jar prepared pasta
   sauce

1 onion, thinly sliced

2 tsp. minced garlic

1 lb. ground beef

1 cup shredded Parmesan
   cheese + more for garnish

1 tsp. red pepper flakes

Salt and pepper to taste

DIRECTIONS:

1. Break spaghetti in half and add to the Instant Pot.

2. Add remaining ingredients except the garnish
   and 6 cups of water to the Instant Pot (I fill the
   pasta sauce jar up with water twice and shake
   it up to remove all the pasta sauce), stirring to
   combine.

3. Secure lid and pressure cook on high for
   10 minutes. Let the pressure release naturally.

4. Remove lid. Fold everything together.

5. Sprinkle with shredded Parmesan cheese.

PUMPKIN-SAGE RAVIOLI

Prep. Time: 45 minutes
Servings: 4–6

INGREDIENTS:

Pasta Dough:

3 cups flour

1 tsp. salt

4 eggs

2 tbsp. olive oil

Pumpkin Filling:

1 cup pumpkin puree

2 tsp. pumpkin-pie spice

1 tsp. finely chopped
   fresh sage

⅓ cup ricotta cheese

1 egg

Salt and pepper to taste

Sage Butter:

4 tbsp. butter

2–3 sage leaves

1 cup water

Vegetable oil spray

Cinnamon

DIRECTIONS:

1. Add flour and salt together in the bowl of a food processor. Pulse to combine. Change food processor blade to dough blade.
2. Whisk eggs and olive oil together. Gradually pour into flour mixture while machine is running to create a soft dough.
3. Remove dough and divide into 2 parts. Allow dough to rest for 10 minutes.
4. In a small bowl add the pumpkin puree, pumpkin pie spice, finely chopped fresh sage, ricotta cheese, and egg. Salt and pepper mixture to your taste, stirring to combine everything. Set aside until ready to use.
5. Roll out each sheet of pasta (¼–⅛-inch thick) and place a small dollop of filling at 2-inch intervals. Place the other sheet of pasta overtop. Press pasta sheet around filling to create the ravioli. Be sure edges are well sealed. Cut into square ravioli shapes and set aside. If you have a favorite ravioli cutter, use it to cut the ravioli.
6. Pour 1 cup water into the Instant Pot.
7. Spray a bamboo steamer basket with vegetable oil spray. Place the prepared ravioli onto the prepared bamboo steamer.
8. Set the bamboo steamer into the Instant Pot.
9. Set the Instant Pot to Steam and steam for 5 minutes. Allow steam to release naturally.
10. In a large sauté pan, melt 4 tbsp. butter and add 2–3 sage leaves.
11. Remove freshly made pumpkin-sage ravioli from the bamboo steamer basket and pan fry them quickly in the sage butter.
12. Serve with a light sprinkling of cinnamon and your favorite sides.

SPAGHETTI AND MEATBALLS

Prep. Time: 45 minutes
Serves: 6–8

INGREDIENTS:

1 lb. ground beef

1 tbsp. minced garlic

1 small red onion, diced

3 tbsp. Italian seasoning herb blend, *divided*

Olive oil

1 lb. spaghetti, broken in half

12 Roma tomatoes, chopped

1 tsp. red pepper flakes

6-oz. can Italian seasoned tomato paste

6 cups water

Freshly chopped basil

Freshly chopped Italian parsley

Freshly grated Parmesan cheese

Salt and pepper to taste

Ricotta cheese, for garnish

DIRECTIONS:

1. In a large bowl, combine beef, garlic, red onion, and 1½ tbsp. Italian seasoning. Mix everything together until combined. Shape into golf ball–sized meatballs and place aside.

2. Heat Instant Pot on Sauté mode. Add enough olive oil to lightly coat bottom of pan. When heated, add meatballs. Do not crowd them. Brown each meatball. If necessary, remove some before adding more, so they aren't crowded while browning. Remove all meatballs when finished.

3. To the Instant Pot add the spaghetti, tomatoes, red pepper flakes, tomato paste, and 6 cups water (mix the tomato paste and water together before adding). Sprinkle with remaining Italian seasoning and place the browned meatballs on top.

4. Secure lid on the pot and pressure cook on high for 10 minutes. Allow pressure to release naturally.

5. Once steam has been released, remove lid and sprinkle with basil, parsley, and Parmesan cheese. Gently fold everything together.

6. Serve with your favorite bread on the side. Put a dollop of ricotta cheese on top of each dish. Salt and pepper to taste.

SEAFOOD

STEAMED MUSSELS

Prep. Time: 30 minutes
Serves: 4–6

INGREDIENTS:

2 lb. mussels

1 cup white wine

1 cup chicken stock

4 tbsp. butter, melted

⅓ cup freshly chopped chives

½ cup finely chopped parsley

⅓ cup finely chopped red bell pepper

⅓ cup finely chopped onion

1 tbsp. freshly minced garlic

Salt and pepper to taste

Lemons, for garnish

DIRECTIONS:

1. Inspect the mussels when purchasing and if any are not tightly sealed, discard them and don't purchase those.

2. Place mussels in large bowl of cold water. Change water every 30 minutes for 2–3 hours. Mussels will filter in clean water and discard the dirt inside of them.

3. When mussels have been cleaned, place in the Instant Pot.

4. Pour white wine and chicken stock over mussels. Add melted butter.

5. Add the rest of ingredients except for lemon and, using a large spoon, stir gently to combine.

6. Secure the lid on the Instant Pot and select the Steam mode. Steam for 10 minutes. Allow pressure to release naturally.

7. Remove lid. Any mussel that hasn't opened should be discarded.

8. Heat large sauté pan on the stove. Spray with vegetable oil.

9. Slice lemons into halves. Pan sear the cut side of lemons to caramelize.

10. Serve mussels in shallow bowls with broth. Place pan-seared lemon halves on side.

THE EVERYDAY INSTANT POT COOKBOOK

BACON-WRAPPED SCALLOPS

Prep. Time: 30 minutes
Serves: 4–6

INGREDIENTS:

1½ lb. scallops

1 pkg. bacon

Salt and pepper to taste

1 cup vegetable stock

¼ cup olive oil

2 garlic cloves, peeled

¼ cup brown sugar

2 limes

DIRECTIONS:

1. Wrap each scallop with bacon. Secure with toothpick.

2. Place prepared scallops on baking sheet. Sprinkle with salt and pepper. Set aside until ready to use.

3. Place steam rack in bottom of the Instant Pot. Layer bacon-wrapped scallops on top of each other.

4. Pour vegetable stock into the Instant Pot and secure the lid.

5. Set Instant Pot on Steam and steam for 10 minutes. Allow steam to release naturally.

6. Place olive oil, garlic cloves, and brown sugar in a food processor. Pulse to combine.

7. Remove bacon-wrapped scallops from Instant Pot. Place on baking sheet.

8. Brush each scallop with olive oil mixture. Squeeze juice of one lime over them.

9. Place scallops under broiler for 4 minutes, or until they start to turn golden brown. Turn scallops once while under broiler.

10. Remove scallops from broiler. Squeeze juice from second lime over them. Serve with your favorite sides.

STEAMED BROCCOLI AND SALMON

Prep. Time: 30 minutes
Serves: 2

INGREDIENTS:

1 cup vegetable stock

2 salmon fillets (8 oz. each)

Salt and pepper to taste

4 lemon slices

4 stalks fresh thyme

2 cups broccoli florets

½ cucumber, seeded and
  finely chopped

5 radishes, finely chopped

1 tbsp. soy sauce

1 tbsp. apple cider vinegar

1 tbsp. olive oil

DIRECTIONS:

1. Pour vegetable stock into the Instant Pot and add the steam rack.

2. Rinse salmon fillets. Place them on the steam rack. Sprinkle salmon fillets with salt and pepper.

3. Arrange lemon slices and thyme stalks on top of salmon fillets.

4. Place broccoli florets around the two salmon fillets. Secure lid on the Instant Pot, select the Steam mode, and steam for 3 minutes. Let steam release naturally.

5. Combine cucumber and radishes in a small bowl. Add soy sauce, apple cider vinegar, olive oil, salt and pepper to taste. Stir to combine.

6. Serve steamed salmon and broccoli with the cucumber and radish relish.

THE EVERYDAY INSTANT POT COOKBOOK

STEAMED SHRIMP

Prep. Time: 30 minutes
Serves: 8–10

INGREDIENTS:

2 lb. 16/20 shrimp, peeled and thawed

1 cup white wine

¼ cup fresh lemon juice

¼ cup Dijon mustard

¼ cup mayonnaise

1 lemon, sliced, for garnish

DIRECTIONS:

1. Clean shrimp by shelling and deveining them. If frozen, thaw by placing the shrimp in a large bowl and run cold water over them for 5 to 10 minutes.

2. Place steam tray into the Instant Pot. Place shrimp on top.

3. Pour white wine and fresh lemon juice into Instant Pot. Secure lid.

4. Select Steam mode and steam for 3 minutes. Let steam release naturally. Remove lid.

5. Place the shrimp in a single layer on a small baking dish. Place in refrigerator to chill.

6. Mix Dijon mustard and mayonnaise together.

7. When shrimp are chilled, serve with Dijon mustard mixture. Garnish with freshly sliced lemon.

SAUCES/ MISCELLANEOUS

PIZZA SAUCE/SPAGHETTI SAUCE

Prep. Time: 45 minutes
Serves: 6–8

INGREDIENTS:

10 Roma tomatoes, chopped

1 tbsp. Italian seasoning herb blend

1 large yellow onion, chopped

6 garlic cloves

6-oz. can tomato paste

2 cups water

Salt and pepper to taste

DIRECTIONS:

1. Add everything into Instant Pot. Secure lid.

2. Pressure cook on high for 30 minutes. Let steam release naturally. Remove lid.

3. Using a blender, puree sauce in small batches. Adjust salt and pepper to taste. Be very careful; hot sauce will expand when blended and could potentially splash and burn you.

4. Once the sauce is prepared, use it on your favorite homemade pizza or with One-Pot Spaghetti recipe (page 121).

HARD-BOILED EGGS

Prep. Time: 5 minutes
Serves: 4–6

INGREDIENTS:

Water

1–12 Eggs

DIRECTIONS:

1. To hard-boil eggs, add 1 cup of water to your Instant Pot and place the steam rack into the pot.

2. Carefully place one to a dozen eggs on top of the steam rack.

3. Pressure cook on high for 5 minutes. When the time finishes, allow the eggs to sit for 5 minutes before doing a quick release on the pressure.

4. Carefully move the eggs to a cold bowl of water and allow them sit in cold water for at least 5 minutes.

5. When the eggs are cool enough to peel, prepare and add hard-boiled eggs as indictated in the recipe directions

HOMEMADE YOGURT

Prep. Time: 10 hours
Serves: Variable

INGREDIENTS:

1 gallon whole milk

¼ cup fruit pectin

2 cups plain yogurt

1 cup hulled and cleaned
strawberries, *optional*

1 large banana, *optional*

DIRECTIONS:

1. Pour 1 gallon of milk and fruit pectin into Instant Pot.

2. Set to Sauté mode. Stir gently until it reaches 180°F. Turn off Instant Pot. Let milk cool to room temperature.

3. Add 2 cups plain yogurt. Stir to mix.

4. Secure lid on Instant Pot. Select Yogurt mode. Press start.

5. When finished, remove lid.

6. Make a smoothie by blending 2 cups of freshly made yogurt with strawberries and banana.

OLD-FASHIONED HOT FUDGE

Prep. Time: 45 minutes
Serves: 12

INGREDIENTS:

2 cups sugar

¼ cup flour

⅔ cup cocoa powder

2 cups whole milk

4 tbsp. butter

1 tbsp. vanilla extract

DIRECTIONS:

1. In Instant Pot, combine sugar, flour, and cocoa powder. Whisk dry ingredients together. If making gluten-free, simply omit flour and add 1½ tbsp. cornstarch.

2. Select Sauté mode and add milk and butter. Bring fudge to a boil while stirring gently. Let boil for 2 minutes.

3. Turn off Instant Pot. Add vanilla, stirring to incorporate.

4. Let sauce cool slightly. Serve with your favorite dessert dishes.

THE EVERYDAY INSTANT POT COOKBOOK

CARAMEL RUM SAUCE

Prep. Time: 20 minutes
Serves: Variable

INGREDIENTS:

2 cups heavy cream

2 cups brown sugar

1 tsp. rum extract

DIRECTIONS:

1. Combine all ingredients into Instant Pot. Stir together.

2. Pressure cook on high for 10 minutes. Let pressure release naturally. Remove lid.

3. If caramel color isn't deep enough, select Sauté mode and boil until mixture has reached desired color.

BUBBLE TEA

Prep. Time: 30 minutes
Serves: 6–8

INGREDIENTS:

10 cups water

1 cup brown sugar

2 cups boba tapioca pearls

4 cups brewed black tea

4 tbsp. sweetened
   condensed milk

Ice, *optional*

DIRECTIONS:

1. Add water, brown sugar, and boba tapioca pearls to Instant Pot. Secure lid and pressure cook on low for 8 minutes. When finished, allow pressure to release naturally.

2. Once pressure is released, remove the lid and stir the tapioca pearls.

3. Carefully spoon ½ cup of boba tapioca pearls into your glass. Fill the glass almost full with brewed tea.

4. Finish off each glass with a large spoonful each of sweetened condensed milk. Stir everything together.

5. If desired, serve over ice.

DESSERTS

COCONUT CHERRY COBBLER

Prep. Time: 60 minutes
Serves: 10–12

INGREDIENTS:

3 cups flour

1½ cups sugar, *divided*

1 tsp. salt

2 tsp. baking powder

1½ cups coconut milk

2 eggs

1 tbsp. vanilla extract

¼ cup olive oil

4 tbsp. butter

1 cup sugar

4 cups fresh pie cherries, pitted

DIRECTIONS:

1. In medium bowl, add flour, ½ cup sugar, salt, and baking powder, whisking everything together to combine. Set aside.

2. In another bowl, combine coconut milk, eggs, vanilla, and olive oil. Whisk together to combine.

3. Add coconut milk mixture to flour mixture. Stir to combine. If necessary, use additional coconut milk to create a thick pancake-like batter. Set aside.

4. Select Sauté mode on the Instant Pot.

5. Add butter and melt while gently stirring. Once butter is melted, add 1 cup sugar. Mix together.

6. Add freshly pitted pie cherries to the butter and sugar. Sauté for 2–3 minutes.

7. Pour cobbler batter over cherries. Secure Instant Pot. Set mode to Cake. Press start.

8. When finished, let pressure release naturally. Remove lid.

9. Serve warm with your favorite ice cream.

AUNT MINNIE'S APPLESAUCE WITH SWEET DUMPLINGS

Prep. Time: 30 minutes
Serves: 6–8

INGREDIENTS:

10–12 apples (I like McIntosh or Golden Delicious)

1 tbsp. cinnamon

1 tsp. nutmeg

2–3 cups sugar (can use more for a sweeter applesauce)

½ tsp. salt

Dumplings:

2 cups all-purpose flour

1 tbsp. baking powder

4 tbsp. cold butter

½ cup sugar

1 cup milk (may need a little extra)

DIRECTIONS:

1. Peel and core apples. Slice into wedges and place into the Instant Pot.

2. Add cinnamon, nutmeg, sugar, ½ cup water, and salt. Stir to combine.

3. Secure Instant Pot lid. Pressure cook on high for 5 minutes. Let pressure release naturally. Remove lid.

4. Using a potato masher, mash cooked apples into a sauce.

5. Using a food processor, add flour, baking powder, butter, and sugar. Pulse together until butter is cut into flour, and mixture resembles coarse cornmeal.

6. Transfer flour mixture into mixing bowl. Add milk.

7. Using a fork, gently mix milk and flour mixture together until it combines into a wet dough. If needed, add more milk to achieve a wet dough.

8. Add 1 cup water to applesauce and stir together. Spoon-drop prepared dumplings on top of the applesauce.

9. Secure Instant Pot lid. Select Steam mode and steam for 5 minutes. Let pressure release naturally. Remove lid.

10. Spoon dumplings and applesauce into small bowl. Pour some cream over the top and enjoy!

SWEET STICKY RICE WITH MANGO

Prep. Time: 1 hour
Serves: 6–8

INGREDIENTS:

Coconut Sauce:

2 cups coconut milk

½ cup sugar

½ tsp. salt

1 tbsp. rice flour

Sweet Sticky Rice:

2 cups sweet rice

3 cups coconut milk

¾ cup sugar

½ tsp. salt

3–4 ripe mangoes, for garnish

DIRECTIONS:

1. To make the sauce, add coconut milk, sugar, salt, and rice flour to Instant Pot and select the Sauté mode.

2. Bring to boil while gently stirring. Let mixture thicken. Remove sauce from the Instant Pot and set aside.

3. To make the rice, add the sweet rice and 3 cups water to the Instant Pot. Select Rice mode. Press start.

4. Once rice is cooked, remove the lid and add 3 cups coconut milk, sugar, and salt to cooked rice. Secure the lid and steam for 5 minutes. Let the steam release naturally before removing the lid.

5. Peel and slice fresh mango to serve on side.

6. To serve, place a large spoonful of sweet sticky rice on plate with some fresh mango on the side. Drizzle with the coconut sauce.

BREAD PUDDING
WITH A CARAMEL RUM SAUCE

Prep. Time: 4 hours
Serves: 6–8

INGREDIENTS:

4 cups cream

8 eggs

2 tsp. pumpkin-pie spice

½ cup brown sugar

1 tbsp. vanilla extract

½ tsp. salt

8 croissants (crumbled into
    coarse pieces)

DIRECTIONS:

1. In the inner pot of the Instant Pot, combine cream, eggs, pumpkin-pie spice, brown sugar, vanilla, and salt. Whisk together.

2. Add crumbled croissants to the egg mixture, gently folding to combine. Cover inner pot and place in refrigerator for 2–3 hours.

3. Place the inner pot back into the Instant Pot and secure the lid.

4. Select Cake mode and press start. When the Instant Pot is finished, let the steam release naturally. Remove lid.

5. Serve warm with the Caramel Rum Sauce (see page 145).

CHEESECAKE IN A JAR

Prep. Time: 45 minutes
Serves: 4–5

INGREDIENTS:

1 cup sliced strawberries

1 cup raspberries

1 cup blueberries

1 cup blackberries

4 tbsp. apricot jam

2 8-oz. pkgs. cream cheese

5 eggs

¼ cup sour cream

¼ cup cornstarch

1 tsp. almond extract

1 tsp. vanilla extract

2 cups graham cracker crumbs

4 or 5 8-ounce jelly jars

DIRECTIONS:

1. Combine berries in a large bowl. Fold apricot jam into them (it's easier if you warm the jam first). Set aside until ready to use.

2. In a food processor, combine cream cheese, eggs, sour cream, cornstarch, and almond and vanilla extracts; puree until smooth.

3. Gather 4 to 5 widemouthed 8-ounce jelly jars; press ½ inch of graham cracker crumbs into bottom of each. Reserve extra crumbs.

4. Divide and pour the cheesecake batter into each jar, filling ¾ of the way.

5. Place steam rack in bottom of Instant Pot. Pour 1 cup water into the pot.

6. Place prepared cheesecake jars onto the steam rack.

7. Pressure cook on low for 25 minutes. Let steam release naturally. Remove Instant Pot lid. Allow mini-cheesecakes to fully cool.

8. Sprinkle tops with extra graham cracker crumbs. Top with fresh berries mixture.

STEAMED GINGERBREAD

Prep. Time: 60 minutes
Serves: 8–10

INGREDIENTS:

½ cup butter, softened

¼ cup sugar

¼ cup brown sugar

1 large egg

2 cups flour

2 tsp. baking powder

½ tsp. baking soda

¼ tsp. salt

1 tbsp. ground ginger

2 tsp. cinnamon

⅔ cup molasses

⅔ cup milk

Fresh cream for serving

DIRECTIONS:

1. In the bowl of your stand mixer, using the paddle attachment, cream the butter and sugars together for 3 minutes. Once butter and sugars are creamed, add egg. Blend thoroughly.

2. In a separate bowl, combine flour, baking powder, baking soda, salt, ginger, and cinnamon. Whisk together to fully combine. Set aside until ready to use.

3. Measure milk and molasses together; set aside. (I heat the milk and molasses mixture to help them combine easier.)

4. Add dry and wet ingredients (alternating) into the butter mixture until everything is fully incorporated.

5. Spray the inside of a 32-ounce ramekin with vegetable spray. Pour batter into the prepared ramekin. Place the rack into the Instant Pot and pour 1 cup water into the bottom of the pot. Place the ramekin on top of the rack. Set it to Cake mode. Press start. When finished, let steam release naturally. Remove lid.

6. Serve with fresh cream and enjoy!

THE EVERYDAY INSTANT POT COOKBOOK

SWEETENED DUMPLINGS WITH RHUBARB AND FRESH CREAM

Prep. Time: 45 minutes
Serves: 6–8

INGREDIENTS:

4 cups cleaned and sliced rhubarb stalks

1½ cups sugar, *divided*

zest and juice from one orange

zest and juice from one lemon

2 cups flour

2 eggs

½ cup cream, plus more for serving

1 tsp. vanilla extract

¼ tsp. baking powder

½ tsp. salt

Cinnamon, nutmeg, and sugar, for sprinkling

DIRECTIONS:

1. Select Sauté on the Instant Pot.

2. Add rhubarb, 1 cup sugar, and juice and zest from the orange and lemon to the pot.

3. Stir everything together. Bring to boil. Cook until rhubarb is soft and pulpy (about 20 minutes).

4. Combine flour, eggs, ½ cup cream, ½ cup sugar, vanilla, baking powder, and salt in a large bowl. Mix together.

5. Drop dough a spoonful at a time on top of rhubarb. Sprinkle top of dumplings with cinnamon, nutmeg, and sugar.

6. Secure lid. Steam for 10 minutes. Let steam release naturally.

7. Serve rhubarb and dumplings warm with fresh cream poured over top.

ABOUT THE AUTHOR

Photo Credit: Shaun Anders

Chef Bryan Woolley is one of the longest consistently running television chefs in America. He is an American celebrity chef television personality, and operatic tenor with a degree in Music Education from Utah State University. Chef Bryan currently appears and hosts a daily live cooking segment on the Salt Lake City CBS affiliate KUTV Channel 2 at noon, and for years has hosted a weekly 30-minute cooking show, *Cooking with Chef Bryan*, also on KUTV channel 2 and KMYU, digital channel 2.2. Chef Bryan is also the national spokesperson for Green Giant International's potato and onion division, Potandon Produce, and reaches millions of people.

In addition to his rigorous public appearance schedule, Chef Bryan offers culinary tours to exotic destinations around the world. He also helped to create and teaches a culinary chemistry course at the University of Utah.

Chef Bryan's mission is to empower the home chef by teaching them how to use fresh ingredients for a more nutritious and diverse culinary experience. All of the recipes he demonstrates on TV or in classrooms can be found on his website at www.cookingwithchefbryan.com.

CONVERSION CHARTS

Metric and Imperial Conversions

(These conversions are rounded for convenience)

Ingredient	Cups/Tablespoons/Teaspoons	Ounces	Grams/Milliliters
Butter	1 cup/ 16 tablespoons/ 2 sticks	8 ounces	230 grams
Cheese, shredded	1 cup	4 ounces	110 grams
Cream cheese	1 tablespoon	0.5 ounce	14.5 grams
Cornstarch	1 tablespoon	0.3 ounce	8 grams
Flour, all-purpose	1 cup/1 tablespoon	4.5 ounces/0.3 ounce	125 grams/8 grams
Flour, whole wheat	1 cup	4 ounces	120 grams
Fruit, dried	1 cup	4 ounces	120 grams
Fruits or veggies, chopped	1 cup	5 to 7 ounces	145 to 200 grams
Fruits or veggies, puréed	1 cup	8.5 ounces	245 grams
Honey, maple syrup, or corn syrup	1 tablespoon	0.75 ounce	20 grams
Liquids: cream, milk, water, or juice	1 cup	8 fluid ounces	240 milliliters
Oats	1 cup	5.5 ounces	150 grams
Salt	1 teaspoon	0.2 ounce	6 grams
Spices: cinnamon, cloves, ginger, or nutmeg (ground)	1 teaspoon	0.2 ounce	5 milliliters
Sugar, brown, firmly packed	1 cup	7 ounces	200 grams
Sugar, white	1 cup/1 tablespoon	7 ounces/0.5 ounce	200 grams/12.5 grams
Vanilla extract	1 teaspoon	0.2 ounce	4 grams

Oven Temperatures

Fahrenheit	Celsius	Gas Mark
225°	110°	1/4
250°	120°	1/2
275°	140°	1
300°	150°	2
325°	160°	3
350°	180°	4
375°	190°	5
400°	200°	6
425°	220°	7
450°	230°	8

INDEX